the Little Book of

SEA & SOUL

the Little Book of

SEA & SOUL

Denise Adams

NIMBUS
PUBLISHING LTD

Nimbus Publishing Limited
3731 Mackintosh St, Halifax, NS B3K 5A5
(902) 455-4286 nimbus.ca

Printed and bound in China

NB1174

All photos by Denise Adams
Design: Jenn Embree

Help us keep the light shining.
For information on fundraising events for the preservation
of our beloved little beacon, Paddy's Head lighthouse, in
Indian Harbour, St. Margarets Bay, Nova Scotia, please email
denisebythesea@eastlink.ca.

Library and Archives Canada Cataloguing in Publication

Adams, Denise, 1961-, author
The little book of sea & soul / Denise Adams.
ISBN 978-1-77108-291-4 (bound)

1. Atlantic Coast (Canada)—Pictorial works. 2. Atlantic
Coast (Canada)—Anecdotes. 3. Marine photography.
I. Title. II. Title: Little book of sea and soul.

FC2005.A33 2015   971.50022'2   C2014-907811-0

Nimbus Publishing acknowledges the financial support for its
publishing activities from the Government of Canada through
the Canada Book Fund (CBF) and the Canada Council for
the Arts, and from the Province of Nova Scotia through Film
& Creative Industries Nova Scotia. We are pleased to work in
partnership with Film & Creative Industries Nova Scotia to
develop and promote our creative industries for the benefit of
all Nova Scotians.

The sea is such a part of me that I can hardly have a thought that doesn't involve it.

Give me a long beach to walk on and I am happy all day.

Anyone can steer a boat in calm seas.

I'd rather have a little window to the sea than fine clothing and jewelry.

Life is full of uncertainty, but if you stayed anchored at all times you would go nowhere.

The only remedy for the homesick Maritimer is a return to the coast.

The sea is much larger and deeper than the sum of its visible parts.

You can never
dip your paddle
in the same
water twice.

I care about the ocean more than I could ever know about it.

If you've thought of putting a message in a bottle but don't know what to send, write: "Help, I'm drowning in plastic."

Fog is lovely for its mysterious ambiance;
it's a pain when there are clothes on the line.

There is much consensus that life began in the ocean.

I go to the ocean first for counsel and healing.

The fountain of youth, I believe, is actually the sea.

Become a sea-hugger.

Never mind the bad weather that comes with living at the coast;
a few fine days will make up for it tenfold.

The immensity of the ocean can make a person feel either lonely or in the company of greatness.

If you don't like crowds, move to a bold coastline.

A rowboat, a church portal, a fish, hands clasped in prayer: interesting that they all share the same basic shape.

True wisdom is to know when not to venture out to sea.

No two waves are alike.

You will not know the ocean's vastness until your boat is so far out that land is no longer in sight.

Go for a walk on the beach in the pouring rain.

Better is the experience of going to the shore when you don't have much time to spare, than only going if you have nothing else to do.

There are worse storms in politics than there are at sea.

The best "quiet time" is spent with a loud pounding surf.

I forget my age when I'm at the beach.

Close your eyes and listen. The sound of the sea is almost indistinguishable from the rolling applause of a standing ovation.

Water cleanses;
the sea heals.

You will never be able to please everyone, so just keep rowing toward your destination.

Big fish eat little fish: that's capitalism in a clamshell.

A regular dose of fresh sea air will add years to your life and life to your years.

It is the sea that gives our planet the appearance of a shimmering blue jewel hanging in space.

Too much time in the wheelhouse can land a man in the doghouse.

If you hate the look of seaweed at low tide, go snorkelling.

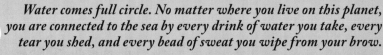

Water comes full circle. No matter where you live on this planet, you are connected to the sea by every drink of water you take, every tear you shed, and every bead of sweat you wipe from your brow.

Behind every keel, there's a good rudder.

Never underestimate the power of the sea.

On those days when I am as restless as the sea, I go to the coast.
There, somehow, I feel understood.

Pleasure for an hour is a glass of wine.
Pleasure for a day is a bouquet of flowers.
Pleasure for life is access to the ocean.

It's been proven that sand between toes relieves stress.

Follow your own compass no matter what others say.

A little house by the sea needs neither art on the walls nor music playing.

I remain hopeful that the beauty and bounty of the sea will awaken the human soul to act on its behalf.

How to tell the tides:

Wet beach:
Tide going out.

Dry beach:
Tide coming in.

Rainy day:
Stick around to find out.

What but the sea appeals to all of the senses at once?

If you feel like you're navigating this life on a drifting raft, hang on to that towline. It will come in handy.

The closest I ever got to having wings was at the edge of a wharf, between a starry moonlit sky and a sparkling still sea.

The French call seafood "fruits de mer," which literally means, fruit of the sea.

Fog challenges our perceptions. It is a reminder that there are always underlining realities that we cannot see.

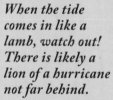

When the tide comes in like a lamb, watch out! There is likely a lion of a hurricane not far behind.

The sound of the ocean trumps all music.

How we treat the ocean is a reflection of our values.

We may indeed be separate islands, but we are joined by a common sea.

*The oceans
are as
secretive as
the heavens.*

"Come-from-aways" come here to play;
locals must leave to find work and pay.

Salty toes are happy toes.

Some events in life are as dark as a troubled sea; rest assured that calm seas and sunshine are always in the forecast at some point.

Not so long ago, it took longer to sail across the Atlantic than it now takes to fly to the moon.

Whoever coined the phrase "don't look back" must not have had the state of the ocean in mind.

If you really have to go out of your way to reach the coast, do yourself a favour: do nothing once you get there.

The ocean is a page-less history book.

*There's a little lighthouse
in each of us.*